MY HUSBAND LEFT ME FOR ANOTHER WOMAN! NOW WHAT?

Healing Journal

Mary Peterson

Copyright © 2021 Mary Peterson

All rights reserved. No part of this publication may be reproduced, distributed, or transmitted in any form or by any means, including photocopying, recording, or other electronic or mechanical methods, without the prior written permission of the publisher.

The information provided within this book is for general information purposes only. While the author tries to keep the information up-to-date and correct, there are no representations or warranties, express or implied about the completeness, accuracy, reliability, suitability or availability with respect to the information, products or services contained in this book for any purpose. Any use of this information is at your own risk. Any advice that is provided in this book is based on the experience of the author. All opinions expressed in this book are solely the opinion of the author.

All Scripture quotations are taken from Life Application
Study Bible (NKJV).
Weaton, Ill: Tyndale House Publishers, Inc., 1993

ISBN: 978-1-7365872-2-5

Guiding Dove, LLC Trademark of Mary Peterson.
Trademarks may be registered in some jurisdictions.
All other trademarks are the property of their respective owners.

Chapter 1-Activity

You're Going to Be Okay!

Fear not, for I am with you; Be not dismayed, for I am your God. I will strengthen you, Yes, I will help you, I will uphold you with my righteous right hand.

—Isaiah 40:10

Write:

1. I am worthy!

   _____

2. I am loved!

   _____

3. I am strong!

   _____

4. I am wise!

   _____

5. I am a precious gift from God and created for a purpose!

   _____

_____

_____

6. There is a reason I am going through this pain!

_____

_____

7. I will be OK!

_____

Chapter 2-Activity

Why Am I Feeling So Much Pain?

For I know the thoughts that I think toward you, says the Lord, thoughts of peace and not of evil, to give you a future and a hope.

—Jeremiah 29:11

1. Write: This is not my fault.

   _____

2. Write the reasons you feel led to your husband leaving you and how it made you feel. (Do not give the reasons he told you. These are your feelings only.)

   _____

   _____

   _____

   _____

   _____

   _____

   _____

   _____

Chapter 3-Activity

You Are One Hundred Percent in Control

Do you not know that you are the temple of God and that the Spirit of God dwells in You?

—1 Corinthians 3:16

Explain in detail how you have been dealing with your pain. What actions have you taken (good & bad) to help heal or numb your pain?

_____
_____
_____
_____
_____
_____
_____
_____
_____
_____
_____

Chapter 4-Activity

First Things First

"Be strong and of good courage, do not fear nor be afraid of them; for the Lord your God, He is the One who goes with you. He will not leave you nor forsake you."

—*Deuteronomy 31:6*

Write a list of actions you need to take to protect yourself physically and financially and the dates you will complete them.

_____

_____

_____

_____

_____

_____

_____

_____

_____

Chapter 5-Activity

The Other Woman

For God has not given us a spirit of fear, but a power and of love and of sound mind.

—2 Timothy 1:7

Make a list of promises to yourself of healthy and wise alternatives to verbalizing and/or thinking about the other woman.

_____

_____

_____

_____

_____

_____

_____

_____

Chapter 6-Activity

The Other Dirty Secret

For all that is in the world-the lust of the flesh, the lust of the eyes, and the pride of the life-is not of the Father but is of the world. And the world is passing away, and the lust of it; but he who does the will of God abides forever.

—*1 John 2:16-17*

If relevant, write down how his pornography and other addictions made you feel and why you think it hurt your marriage.

_____

_____

_____

_____

_____

_____

_____

_____

Chapter 7-Activity

Reconciliation

And above all things have fervent love for one another, for love will cover a multitude of sins. Be hospitable to one another without grumbling.

—*1 Peter 4:8-9*

Write the reasons you would want to reconcile (get back together) with your husband. What would be different to prevent infidelity from happening again?

_____

_____

_____

_____

_____

_____

_____

_____

_____

_____

Chapter 8-Activity

Struggles Make Us Stronger

May the God of all grace, who called us to His eternal glory by Christ Jesus, after you have suffered a while, perfect, establish, strengthen, and settle you. To Him be the glory and the dominion forever and ever.

—Amen. 1 Peter 5:10-11

Write the struggles you have endured that have made you stronger and wiser.

_____

_____

_____

_____

_____

_____

_____

_____

_____

Chapter 9-Activity

Loneliness and Desperation

Be anxious for nothing, but in everything by prayer and supplication, with thanksgiving, let your requests be made known to God; and the peace of God, which surpasses all understanding, will guard your hearts and minds through Christ Jesus.

—Philippians 4:6-7

Write your prayer of all the things you need to SURRENDER to God and ask Him to show you how worthy and loved you truly are.

_____

_____

_____

_____

_____

_____

_____

_____

_____

Chapter 10-Activity

Forgiveness

If we confess our sins, He is faithful and just to forgive us our sins and to cleanse us from all unrighteousness.

—1 John 1:9

Write a list of all the things you need forgiveness of and what you need to forgive your husband and others of.

_____

_____

_____

_____

_____

_____

_____

_____

_____

_____

_____

_____

Chapter 11-Activity

The Children

Behold, children are a heritage from the Lord, the fruit of the womb is a reward.

—Psalm. 127:3

Write down the ways you can help your children ease their pain of your separation from their father and the changes that are and will occur.

_____

_____

_____

_____

_____

_____

_____

_____

_____

Chapter 12-Activity

Child Visitation

But do not forget to do good and to share, for with such sacrifices God is well pleased.

—Hebrews 13:16

Write down a child visitation summary of what yearly schedule will be fair to you, your children, and their father. (This may be a temporary schedule.)

Keep in mind the following holidays:

New Year's Eve & Day
Easter Sunday/Spring School Break
Mother's Day
Father's Day
Independence Day/Summer School Break
Thanksgiving/Fall School Break
Christmas Eve & Day/Winter School Break

_____

_____

_____

_____

Chapter 13-Activity

Divorce

Let all bitterness, wrath, anger, clamor, and evil speaking be put away from you, with all malice. And be kind to one another, tenderhearted, forgiving one another, even as God in Christ forgave you.

—*Ephesians 4:31-32*

Write a detailed list of all the pros and cons of being divorced.

Pros:

_____

_____

_____

_____

_____

_____

_____

_____

Pros (cont.):

_____

_____

_____

_____

Cons:

_____

_____

_____

_____

_____

_____

_____

_____

_____

_____

Chapter 14-Activity

Letting Go

Trust in the Lord with all your heart, and lean not on your own understanding; in all your ways acknowledge Him, and He shall direct your paths.

—Proverbs 3:5-6

Write out your answer to:

What does "Letting Go" mean to me?

_____

_____

_____

_____

_____

_____

_____

_____

_____

Chapter 15-Activity

Living Your Dream

"But seek first the kingdom of God and His righteousness, and all these things shall be added to you."

—*Matthew 6:33*

Answer this question:

If I heal from my pain, after realizing nothing will change if I reconcile with my husband, what does "Living My Dream" look like and what are the steps I can take to make it happen?

_____

_____

_____

_____

_____

_____

_____

_____

Final Activity

Continue to use this Healing Journal to write out your feelings throughout this very temporary time of your healing process.

(When you look back at this journal you will see how much you have overcome and grew into knowing how priceless you are!)

_____

_____

_____

_____

_____

_____

_____

_____

_____

_____

Made in the USA
Middletown, DE
27 March 2024